Understanding Mental Illness:
A Guide for Family and Friends

by

Valerie Allen, Ed.D., NCSP, CCM

~ ~ ~

LARGE PRINT EDITION

ISBN-9798828484065

Amazon.com/dp/B0B1CP8FTP

Understanding Mental Illness:
A Guide for Family and Friends

Valerie Allen
Copyright 2022

Understanding Mental Illness:
A Guide for Family and Friends

(LARGE PRINT EDITION)
by
Valerie Allen, Ed.D., NCSP, CCM

For more information, please contact:

Valerie Allen

DrValerieAllen@gmail.com

DrVAllen.com

VAllenWriter@gmail.com

ValerieAllenWriter.com

Amazon.com/author/valerieallen

ACKNOWLEDGEMENT

Nobody realizes that some people

expend tremendous energy

merely to be normal.

Albert Camus
French Philosopher, Author, Journalist

Contents

CHAPTER ONE:

Mental Illness Defined

The *American Psychiatric Association* (APA) defines Mental Illness as:

Mental illnesses are health conditions involving changes in emotion, thinking, or behavior (or a combination of these). Mental illnesses are associated with distress and/or problems functioning in social, work, or family activities.The National Institute of Mental Health (NIMH) has two classifications of mental illness, *Any Mental Illness* (AMI) and *Serious Mental Illness* (SMI)

1. ***Any Mental Illness (AMI)*** is defined as a mental, behavioral, or emotional disorder. AMI can vary in impact, ranging from no impairment to mild, moderate, and even severe impairment (e.g., individuals with serious mental illness as defined below).

2. ***Serious Mental Illness (SMI)*** is defined as a mental, behavioral, or emotional disorder resulting in serious functional impairment, which substantially interferes with or limits one or more major life activities. The burden of mental illnesses is particularly concentrated among those who experience disability due to SMI.

A mental health condition affects a person's thinking, feeling, behavior and/or mood. These conditions deeply impact day-to-day living and may also impact the ability to relate to others.

A mental health condition isn't the result of one single event. Research suggests multiple, linking causes. Genetics, environment, and lifestyle all can influence whether someone develops a mental health condition. A traumatic life event, a negative childhood, a demanding job, a stressful home life, severe financial problems, and/or a major medical condition, are just a few life-style issues which make some people more emotionally vulnerable and may lead to a mental health condition. There are also biochemical processes, environmental toxins, and basic brain structure, and circuitry which may also play a role.

Mental illness is also referred to as a *mental health disorder,* or *mental health condition.* The term "mental health condition" is used interchangeably in this book.

In the more common vernacular, often called "word on the street," there are many negative references to those with mental health conditions. Some, but not all, of these terms include:

- Crazy
- Crazed
- Emo
- Insane
- Kook
- Kooky
- Loco
- Loony
- Loopy
- Lunatic
- Mad
- Mental
- Nut case
- Nuts
- Nutso
- Nutty
- Psycho

- Schizo
- Squirrely
- Unbalance
- Unhinged
- Wacko
- Wackadoos
- Wacky

CHAPTER TWO:

Signs and Symptoms

Signs and symptoms, although similar, are medically distinctive.

A **Sign** is defined as objective. It is visible, measurable, and/or quantifiable. Signs are observable to self and others. Examples are a cough, a high fever, rash, high blood pressure, bleeding, and so on. The most familiar medical signs are called

Vital Signs. These include body temperature, pulse, blood pressure, and respiration.

A **Symptom** is defined as subjective. It is experienced only by the individual and verbally reported by him or her to others who cannot feel or observe what the person is reporting. Examples are pain, headache, stomach ache, fatigue, and so on.

Signs and symptoms of Mental Health Conditions may manifest in any of the following ways:

- Raised voice, yelling, screaming, argumentative

- Rude, insulting, disrespectful, vulgar, profanity

- Verbal and/or physical threats or intimidation

- Weapons or objects which can be used as a weapon

- Irrational behavior, illogical statements

- Verbal or written plan to carry out a threat/harm to self or others

- Bizarre reports of things seen or heard, smelled or tasted, or sensations

- Inability to calm down; dysregulation of emotions

- Aggressively uncooperative when offered assistance

- Vehement denial of an obvious situation/event

Those with mental health conditions often have, or have a history of these experiences and/or share   these characteristics:

- Emotionally at risk, volatile, vulnerable, naïve

- Paranoid, suspicious, illogical, irrational thinking

- No trust in others, especially authority figures

- Difficulty maintaining employment and/or social relationships

- Raised in poverty

- Limited funds, no insurance

- Unemployed, no benefits

- Few or no employability skills

- Inconsistent employment history

- Dependence on public assistance to survive

- No car, limited access to transportation

- No social support system; alienation from family and friends

- Absence of acceptance, understanding, or affection by others

- Rejection by those who would otherwise be expected to aid, assist, care, cope, or understand

- Negative or hostile acquaintances/friends/associates

- Openly discouraged by others from seeking mental health services

- Limited or no dental, and/or medical health care

- Poor hygiene

- Limited formal education or training

- History of hospitalizations, especially via the ER

- Legal issues, criminal record, a history of incarceration

- They and/or their family or friends are known to local law enforcement

CHAPTER THREE:

Facts and Stats

Mental Health Conditions are prevalent in all cultures and societies and have been documented historically. In modern times in the United States of America Ted Bundy, Charles Manson, David Berkowitz, and Ted Karzynski are just a few of those considered to have suffered from serious mental illness leading to extreme criminal behavior.

Those with a mental health condition are not necessarily violent or aggressive, however, those who have a mental health condition who turn to crime are sensationalized. This leads to a misunderstanding about those with a mental health condition who are productive members of society and law-abiding citizens.

This stigma often keeps those who need mental health services, including therapy and/or medication, from seeking help.

The *National Survey on Drug Use and Health* (NSDUH) defines mental health services as having received in-patient treatment/counseling or out-patient treatment/counseling or having used prescription medication for problems with emotions, nerves, or mental health.

Mental health conditions are classified into two major categories, *Any Mental Illness* (AMI) and *Serious Mental Illness* (SMI) by the National Institute of Mental Health (NIMH)

In 2019 the NIMH estimated that 20.6% of adults in the United States suffered from *Any Mental Illness* (AMI).

The *National Institute of Mental Health* (NIMH) provides the following data about *Any Mental Illness* (AMI) in 2019:

- The prevalence of AMI was higher among females (24.5%) than males (16.3%).

- Young adults aged 18-25 had the highest prevalence of AMI, 29.4%

- Adults aged 26-49 years with AMI was 25.0%

- Those aged 50 and older with AMI was 14.1%

- The prevalence of AMI was highest among adults reporting they were of two or more races 31.7%

- White adults AMI was 22.2%

- The prevalence of AMI was lowest among Asian adults at 14.4%.

In 2019, among the 51.5 million adults with AMI, 23.0 million (44.8%) received mental health services.

- Females, with AMI 49.7%, received mental health services

- Males, with AMI 36.8%, received mental health services

- The percentage of young adults aged 18-25 years with AMI who received mental health services was 38.9%

- Adults with AMI aged 26-49 years who received mental health services was 45.4%

- Those aged 50 and older, who received mental health services was 47.2%.

The National Institute of Mental Health (NIMH) provides the following data in 2019 about *Serious Mental Illness* (SMI) for adults in the U.S:

- Among the 13.1 million adults with SMI, 8.6 million (65.5%) received mental health treatment in the past year.

- More females with SMI (70.5%) received mental health treatment than males with SMI (56.5%).

- The percentage of young adults aged 18-25 years with SMI who received mental health treatment (56.4%) was lower than adults with SMI aged 26-49 years (65.1%) and those aged 50 and older (74.3%).

Diagnostic interview data from the *National Comorbidity Survey Adolescent Supplement* (NCS-A), shows the lifetime prevalence of any mental disorder among U.S. adolescents aged 13-18.

- An estimated 49.5% of adolescents had *Any Mental Illness (AMI)*.

- Of adolescents with mental illness, an estimated 22.2% had severe impairment. DSM-IV based criteria were used to determine impairment level.

Other studies of *Any Mental Illness* (AMI) and *Serious Mental Illness* (SMI) in the United States found:

- 1 in 5 adults experience mental illness each year

- 1 in 6 youth aged 6-17 experience a mental health disorder each year

- 50 % of all lifetime mental illness begins by age 14

- 75% of all lifetime mental illness begins by age 24

CHAPTER FOUR:

Levels of Care

There are three basic levels of care for those with a mental health condition, out-patient therapy, partial hospitalization, and in-patient care.

Out-patient Therapy

Out-patient Therapy (OPT) is the most common use of mental health services. Services are confidential and must be offered by a Licensed Mental Health Professional, which may include a psychiatrist, psychologist, or other legally licensed mental health professional. It is often referred to as "psychotherapy" or "talk therapy." OPT can include the use of prescribed medications by a psychiatrist or a licensed physician. OPT is usually in one hour block sessions, brief in duration, perhaps ongoing for weeks or months, and the focus is specific, based on the patient's needs and situation.

OPT is usually covered by insurance or an employee assistance program (EAP). Typically, insurance will require a deductible and a co-payment, with no limit on the number of sessions allowed. Some require that the licensed professional is within their network of providers.

An Employee Assistance Program (EAP) is offered by the employer as part of the employee's fringe benefit package. An EAP is not insurance, as such, there is no deductible and no co-payment, however, the number of sessions is limited. An EAP usually allows from six to ten sessions, some offer more and some offer less. An EAP is considered brief, focused therapy by a licensed mental health professional.

Out-patient therapy typically is offered locally and conducted at the patient's request. His or her concerns are usually about difficulty adjusting to life changes. These may create stress, leading to feeling anxious or depressed. These emotions can become overwhelming and result in poor coping skills and/or bad judgment. This in turn can impact on functioning and interfere with activities of daily living, including school, work, finances, personal relationships, family responsibilities, physical health, and other obligations.

Out-Patient Therapy (OPT)

- Is the most frequently used mental health care

- Provides services to an individual, couple, children/teens, or families

- May be done in groups with a specific need, i.e., grieving, blended families, divorce, retirement, coping with medical conditions, addictions, anger management, and so on

- Is the most effective in a brief amount of time

- Is the least expensive mental health care

- Is the most convenient

- Is the least intrusive

- Is usually a voluntary request by the individual

- Can be required by a training program or institution of higher learning to be accepted into or maintained in a course of study

- Can be mandatory by an employer to maintain employment

- Can be court ordered to fulfill legal obligations

- Can be required prior to medical procedures

Partial Hospitalization

Partial hospitalization, sometimes referred to as a "day program," is available on two levels, Partial Hospitalization Programs (PHP) or Intensive Out-Patient Care (IOP)

Partial Hospitalization Programs (PHP), also known as "day programs," refer to out-patient programs that patients attend for six or more hours a day, every day or most days of the week. These programs, which are less intensive than in-patient hospitalization, may focus on psychiatric illnesses, self-harm behaviors, and/or substance abuse. They commonly offer group therapy, educational sessions, and individual counseling.

Intensive Out-Patient Programs (IOP) are similar to PHPs, but are only attended for three to four hours and often meet during evening hours to accommodate persons who are employed. Most IOPs focus on either substance abuse or specific mental health issues, such as Obsessive- Compulsive Disorders, Panic Attacks, Anorexia, or other conditions.

Collectively, these are both a type of intensive out-patient care programs which may be part of a hospital's services or at a free standing facility.

Intensive Out-Patient Care

Intensive Out-patient Care (IOP) are treatment programs used to address specific mental health conditions, such as, addictions, depression, non-suicidal self-harm, anxiety, phobias, eating disorders, or dependencies that do not require detoxification or round-the-clock supervision. Intensive Out-Patient Care enables patients to continue with their normal, day-to-day lives, and live at home. These programs are sometimes covered under insurance.

An intensive out-patient program is a form of partial hospitalization to treat those who would benefit from more support than is provided through standard out-patient therapy but do not require 24-hour in-patient care.

Additionally, an individual who is leaving a 24-hour in-patient treatment environment, such as residential rehabilitation hospitalization, may wish to "step down" to IOP treatment to receive continued intensive support during the day as they make the potentially difficult transition to living at home.

While the exact number of hours of treatment may vary depending upon a person's needs and the particular program, many intensive out-patient programs provide at least nine hours of treatment each week spread out over three to five days, for up to 90 days. Some offer daily programs which last a full day, similar to a school or work routine. Most programs meet on weekdays. Some centers have day and evening programs that usually meet for three hours each.

Most IOPs begin with an assessment of the person's symptoms and living situation. A therapist then creates an individualized program for the person based on their particular needs. The person works with the therapist to create a schedule of how many days and hours they will attend the program each week. This schedule can be adjusted depending on how the person progresses through the program.

IOP treatment offers a range of services to help address specific mental health issues, including:

- Intensive group and individual therapy sessions to learn coping skills, practice better ways to communicate, resolve conflict, and gain an awareness of unhealthy thoughts, beliefs, and behaviors and ways to modify them.

- Medication management, where a physician evaluates a person and determines whether he or she would benefit from medications to treat drug and alcohol withdrawal, reduce cravings, decrease anxiety, overcome depression, or treat other mental health issues.

- Case management, which can assist with connecting to community resources, special education programs, job training, housing, and/or healthcare.

- Enhanced services, such as K-12 classes, childcare, transportation, housing and meals, parenting education, tobacco cessation treatment, recreational activities, and alternative therapies like mindfulness, and acupuncture.

IOPs provide intensive treatment each day for several weeks or months, yet allows participants the freedom to return home to their responsibilities between sessions. This provides them with an opportunity to encounter the inevitable triggers and other stressful situations in everyday life and enables them to practice relapse prevention and coping skills. IOPs may become gradually less intensive as a person progresses in their recovery. Once a person has met their treatment goals, they may transition to a relatively lower level of care, such as standard weekly out-patient therapy or counseling.

There are many individual goals of an IOP, but the overall plan focuses on:

- Increase problem-solving and coping skills for anxiety and depressive symptoms

- Help achieve and maintain abstinence from drugs, alcohol, self-harm, and/or other negative behaviors.

- Support lifestyle changes that promote general well-being.

- Increase participation in support groups.

- Develop a positive support system.

- Help address other psycho-social problems, such as unemployment and legal issues.

- Create relapse prevention skills to develop ways to deal with cravings and/or triggers of highly emotional and/or behavioral responses.

In-Patient Hospitalization

Residential treatment requires clients to reside on site and are actually admitted to the hospital. This is usually covered by insurance.

These hospitals provide assessments, stabilization, and rehabilitation for those who are actively experiencing uncontrolled symptoms of mental disorders such as depression, bipolar disorder, eating disorder, addictions, self-harm, threats to others, and similar conditions.

In-patient hospitalization provides treatment for more severely ill mental health patients, usually for less than 30 days. A person admitted to an in-patient setting might be in the acute phase of mental illness and need help and monitoring around the clock.

In-patient care is not designed to keep individuals confined indefinitely; the goal is to maximize independent living by using the appropriate level of care for a specific illness. Upon discharge the patient's care is turned back over to their treating primary care physician or psychiatrist. Those who are able, may want to consider creating a *Psychiatric Advance Directive* before going to the hospital.

This level of care may be indicated by the following:

- A need for further in-depth assessment
- A safety risk for the individual due to self harming or threats of suicide
- A risk of harm to others

Psychiatric Residential Centers are tailored to meet the needs of those with a chronic psychiatric disorder, such as schizophrenia, bipolar disorder, or psychotic episodes. It is also for those who have a dual diagnosis (i.e., a mental disorder and substance abuse problems), which impairs their ability to function independently.

Voluntary and Involuntary Hospitalization

An individual can choose to voluntarily obtain care, remain in care, or commit to ongoing in-patient and/or out-patient care. However, after a certain number of hours or days, a patient can refuse to cooperate with further medical treatment.

Law Enforcement Officers, Licensed Medical Professionals, and Licensed Mental Health Professionals can only commit patients against their will during extreme cases of psychiatric emergencies. Each state develops its own rules and regulations regarding voluntary and involuntary commitments.

A psychiatric emergency is defined by the *American Psychiatric Association* as "an acute disturbance in thought, behavior, mood, or social relationship, which requires immediate intervention as defined by the patient, family, or social unit."

If a patient with an active psychiatric disorder or who is gravely disabled is exhibiting behaviors that a licensed health care professional believes could lead to imminent harm to that person or another person, then that health care provider can initiate the process of involuntary hospitalization.

Involuntary commitment is typically required if the individual is an imminent danger to self or others, is grossly impaired; and/or behavioral or medical care needs are unmanageable at any available lower level of care. Active family involvement is important unless clinically contraindicated.

Help is available for those in need

- Call 911

- Call 1-800-273-TALK (8255)

- Text MHA to 741741

- Call Domestic Violence 1 (800) 799-7233

- Call LGBTQ 1 (866) 488-7386

- Go to an Urgent Care Center

- Go to the nearest hospital emergency room

- Find a local Community Mental Health Center

- Find a private Licensed Mental Health Professional

CHAPTER FIVE:

Treatment With Medications

There are three basic treatment approaches which have been found to be effective for those with mental health conditions. Use of medications under the care of a physician, typically a psychiatrist, therapy by a licensed mental health professional, typically a psychologist, and a positive social support group, typically family and friends.

The goals of treatment are to minimize signs and symptoms, improve coping abilities, increase logical thought, and engage in rational behavior.

Psychiatry and Medication

Although any licensed physician can prescribe medications, a psychiatrist is a licensed medical physician (MD or DO) who specializes in mental health conditions, including substance use disorders.

Psychiatrists are qualified to assess both the mental and physical aspects of psychological problems. Psychiatric care with medications, known as psychotropic drugs, are an effective adjunct to psychotherapy.

These prescribed medications are approved before use by the *Food and Drug Administration (FDA)* This government agency is responsible for protecting the public health by ensuring the safety, efficacy, and security of human and veterinary drugs, biological products, and medical devices and by ensuring the safety of our nation's food supply, cosmetics, and products that emit radiation.

- Psychotropic medications relate to drugs that affect a person's mental state, emotions, and/or behaviors. They are prescribed to treat a variety of mental health conditions when they cause significant impairment to healthy functioning.

- Psychotropic medications typically work by changing or balancing important chemicals in the brain called neurotransmitters.

- These medications have been approved by the Food and Drug Administration FDA) for their intended use. They can only be prescribed by licensed medical professionals.

- Psychotropic drugs, not prescribed by a licensed physician, intended to be used to affect a person's mental state, emotions, and/or behaviors, includes home remedies, over-the-count medications, natural herbs/supplements, street drugs, and illegal substances. These are not tested nor approved by the Food and Drug Administration and their use can cause serious side effects, illness, death, and/or criminal charges.

- There are five major classes of legal psychotropic medications:
    1. anti-anxiety agents
    2. anti-depressants
    3. anti-psychotics
    4. mood stabilizers
    5. stimulants

Many psychotropic drugs are not designed to work instantly. For some, the medications can take several weeks to have their full effect. Some individuals may need to try several different medications before finding the right one. Many times the dosage of each medication must be frequently adjusted and readjusted.

It is also critical to monitor the person for contraindications. Contraindications are anything, including a symptom or medical condition, that is a reason for a person to not receive a particular treatment, procedure, or medication because it may be harmful.

Everyone responds to medication differently. Side effects should be reported to the treating physician immediately.

Some of the more common side effects of psychotropic medications include:

- Anaphylactic Shock

- Cardiac issues

- Changes in appetite

- Dizziness

- Drowsiness

- Fatigue

- Sexual side effects

- Sleep disturbances

- Weight gain or loss

Barriers to Successful Medication and Psychiatric Treatment

- Limited number of available treating professionals

- Lack of transportation

- No means of payment for services

- Criticism from family and/or friends

- Embarrassment or fear of being "crazy"

- Missed or canceled appointments

- Refusal to take medications as prescribed

- Noncompliance with medication routines and/or dosage

- Discontinuing medications due to a lack of immediate relief or results

- When the condition improves, stopping medication prematurely

CHAPTER SIX: THERAPY

Treatment with Psychotherapy

Psychotherapy is the treatment of mental disorders by psychological rather than medical means. It's often used in combination with medications.

Psychotherapists use talk therapy to treat people for emotional problems and mental health conditions. Depending on what degree and specialty they have, psychotherapists can be psychiatrists, psychologists, counselors, or social workers.

They must be licensed mental health professionals. They can work with individuals, couples, groups, or families.

Often referred to as "talk therapy," the focus may be on problem solving, learning specific techniques for coping with or avoiding problem areas, and identify and change troubling thoughts and/or behaviors.

Counseling is usually short term, specific, and situation focused. Psychotherapy tends to be more long-term than counseling and focuses on a broader range of issues, maladaptive behaviors, poor coping skills, and underlying causes. For some people, these issues are complex and may result in a dual diagnosis with overlapping conditions.

Those in therapy will meet with a therapist to talk. The therapist will ask questions and listen to how the person responds. This helps the therapist know what the real needs and issues are. Therapy helps people learn to cope better, improve communication, and do better overall in life.

Once the person is no longer in crisis, the therapist will help with ongoing support to encourage the positive changes that are being developed and used.

There are different approaches to psychotherapy. However, the four basic forms most commonly used are Psychodynamic, Cognitive-behavioral, Humanistic, and Eclectic.

Psychodynamic Therapy

Psychodynamic Therapy focuses on the psychological roots of emotional suffering. Its hallmarks are self-reflection, self-examination, and the use of the relationship between therapist and patient as a window into problematic relationship patterns in the patient's life.

Psychodynamic therapy involves the interpretation of mental and emotional processes rather than focusing on behavior.

Psychodynamic therapists attempt to help the person find patterns in their emotions, thoughts, beliefs, and behaviors to gain insight into their current self.

Psychodynamic therapy focuses on unconscious processes as they are manifested in the client's present behavior. The goals of psychodynamic therapy are client self-awareness and understanding of the influence of the past on present behavior.

Key features of the Psychodynamic approach are:

- Our behavior and feelings as adults are rooted in our childhood experiences.

- Relationships (particularly parenting) are of primary importance in determining how we feel and behave.

Cognitive-Behavioral Therapy (CBT)

Cognitive-Behavioral Therapy is the most common type of therapy. The goal is for the client to understand internal monologue, build cognitive awareness, and realize how thoughts have an impact on his or her mental state, emotions, and behavior.

CBT therapists emphasize what is going on in the person's current life, rather than what has led up to their difficulties. CBT can help people reduce stress, cope with complicated relationships, deal with grief, and face many other common life challenges.

There are three main components in cognitive behavioral therapy: cognitive therapy, behavioral therapy, and mindfulness-based therapies.

- Cognitive therapy is typically short term and focuses mainly on thought patterns as responsible for negative emotional and behavioral patterns.

- Cognitive behavioral therapy uses exercises in the session as well as "homework" exercises outside of sessions. Clients are helped to develop coping skills, to learn how to change their own thinking, problematic emotions, and behavior. It assists people to find new ways to behave by changing their thought patterns.

- Mindfulness is a type of meditation in which you focus on being intensely aware of what you're sensing and feeling in the moment, without interpretation or judgment. Practicing mindfulness involves breathing methods, guided imagery, and other practices to relax the body and mind and help reduce stress.

Cognitive Behavioral Therapy (CBT) focuses on:

- Targeting and solving current problems

- Challenging and changing cognitive distortions and behaviors

- Improving emotional regulation

- Development of personal coping strategies

Humanistic Therapy

Humanistic Therapy is a mental health approach that emphasizes the importance of being your true self to lead the most fulfilling life. It's based on the principle that everyone has their unique way of looking at the world.

Rather than concentrating on dysfunction, humanistic psychology strives to help people fulfill their potential and maximize their well-being.

Humanistic therapy aims to help clients develop a stronger, healthier sense of self, as well as access and understand their feelings to gain a sense of the meaning of life.

Some of the major concepts and ideas that emerged from the humanistic therapy approach include:

- Person-centered therapy

- Hierarchy of needs.

- Unconditional positive regard.

- Free will.

- Self-concept.

- Self-actualization.

- Peak experiences.

- Fully-functioning person.

Eclectic Therapy

Eclectic therapy is an approach that draws on multiple theoretical orientations and techniques. It is a flexible and multifaceted approach to therapy that allows the therapist to use the most effective methods available to address each individual's needs. This means choosing methods and techniques from different schools of thought to produce positive results and a tailored plan for a specific individual.

Goals of Individual Therapy

The goals of psychotherapy include strengthening the mind, enlarging the capacity of the conscious mind, enabling a person to use their full mental potential, bringing contentment and inner happiness, improving concentration, and increasing willpower to consider alternatives and make better choices.

Research and multiple studies have found that psychotherapy helps people make positive changes in their lives. Reviews of these studies show that about 75% of people who enter psychotherapy show some benefit.

Regardless of the approach used, the benefits of individual therapy may include:

- Improved communication skills.

- A feeling of empowerment.

- Development of insights about life.

- Ability to make healthier choices.

- Use of coping strategies to manage distress.

- Having positive relationship skills.

- Understanding and achieving personal goals.

- Overcoming illnesses such as depression, compulsive behaviors, and eating disorders.

- Boosting self-confidence.

- Overall mood improvement

- Replacing negative thinking with positive thinking.

Barriers to Successful Psychotherapy

- Limited number of available treating professionals

- Lack of transportation

- No means of payment for services

- Criticism/lack of support from family and/or friends

- Embarrassment or fear of being diagnosed

- Missed or canceled appointments

- No motivation to take on responsibility or actively participate in counseling sessions

- Continuing to engage in unhealthy habits and/or toxic relationships

- Noncompliance with recommendations, suggested reading, educational assignments, interactions with others, building a positive social network, etc.

CHAPTER SEVEN:

Positive Social Support Systems

A positive social support system provides structure, routines, and consistency in our relationships and our community. It meets our need for love, acceptance, belonging, and safety. A positive social support system is free of bias, anger, discontent, rejection, and violence.

Infants are simply born into an environment that is either supportive or hostile. The newborn has no choice in their nationality, race, religion, family, or social network.

Children raised by those who are in good health, value education, have financial security, and positive values are more likely to do well during their childhood and find satisfaction and success as adults. Some of their noticeable characteristics include:

- Respect for authority, parents, teachers, law enforcement

- Willing to follow rules and routines
- Accept responsibility for chores, homework, etc.

- Close relationship with family

- Choosing friends with strong ethics and morality

- Completing high school or a GED

- Setting goals and taking action to reach them

- Being kind, compassionate, and considerate of others

Many individuals stray in a negative direction at an early age. This may be due to a lack of supportive parenting, medical conditions, poverty, poor choices, bad decisions, and/or other issues in his or her life. This type of environment often leads to:

- Lack of education; poor academic performance

- School drop out

- Poor health and hygiene

- Financial insecurity

- Aggression and violence

- Resistance to authority on any level

- Lack of trust, fears, suspicions, paranoia

- Alienation from family and friends

- Unacceptable or inappropriate social behavior

- Criminal activity

- A history of rejection by others through neglect by parents/family, teasing and/or bullying

- Building a network of friends with negative or antisocial behaviors

- A lack of motivation or interest in a satisfying career; no future plans or goals

- No ambition; self criticism, a negative self concept, a lack of self confidence

CHAPTER EIGHT:

Licensed Mental Health Professionals

All states have licensing requirements for mental health professionals. This includes specific university level courses, level of educational degrees, post graduate internships, and a passing score on state licensing examinations. Additionally, some require a period of supervision under a fully licensed professional before being allowed to be an independent practitioner.

Many licensed mental health professionals also have national board certifications in specialty areas. Specialties could be by age, that is treating children, teens, young adults, and/or the geriatric population. Specialties could be by issue, such as additions, grieving, divorce marriage counseling, anxiety, depression, or chronic disorders.

Licensed mental health professionals include:

- Psychiatrists (MD or DO) are physicians who specialize in brain chemistry. They can prescribe medication and may offer supportive counseling. As physicians, they understand medical conditions which might have an impact on the individual's mental well-being. This is especially important if a person is taking medications for a medically diagnosed illness or chronic condition.

- Psychologists (Ph.D., Psy.D., Ed.D.) are licensed at the doctoral level of education. They are not physicians but rather specialize in understanding the mind. Their specific skills and education focus on the individual's psyche. Psychologists take into consideration the person's thoughts, emotions, and behaviors. They are familiar with medications and medical conditions which can manifest in signs and symptoms of a mental condition. They often specialize in working with a specific age, population, or condition.

- Other qualified licensed mental health professionals at the master's degree level may include: Licensed Clinical Social Workers (LCSW), Licensed Mental Health Counselors (LMHC), Licensed Marriage and Family Therapists (LMFT). Some states also license Sex Therapists, Pastoral Counselors, and Rehabilitation Counselors.

Non-licensed Individuals

Non-licensed individuals may be helpful and bring comfort to those suffering from temporary distress or chronic mental health conditions, however, they are not licensed mental health professionals.

Even with the best intentions these individuals can pose a threat to the well-being of those who are emotionally at risk. People who are emotionally vulnerable often feel desperate for assistance from any source and will turn to non-licensed individuals for support. This can be financially costly and psychologically damaging.

Non-licensed individuals, in an effort to offer help and relieve suffering, are not licensed mental health professionals and should not try to offer mental health care.

.   These persons may include:
- bartenders
- classmates
- co-workers

- family members
- fortune tellers
- friends
- hair dressers/barbers
- herbalists
- job coaches
- lawyers
- neighbors
- palm readers
- pastoral counselors
- probation officers
- relatives
- religious leaders
- snake oil sales people
- tea leaf readers

Educational Degrees vs Licensure vs Certification

Higher education is beyond a high school level of formal education. There are generally five degrees within higher education programs. These include the

Associate Degree (AA or AS), The Bachelor Degree (BA or BS, The Master's Degree (MA, MS, M.Ed), The Specialists Degree (Sp.D.), and The Doctorate Degree (Ph.D., Psy.D., Ed.D.)

Associate Degree
- Two years of college education
- Usually at a community or state college
- AA = Associate of Arts, a general college degree
- AS = Associate in Science, in a specific vocational area (nurse, firefighter, paralegal, dental hygienist, law enforcement, physical therapy assistance, and so on.)

Bachelor's Degree
- Two years of formal education beyond the Associate Degree
- Four years of formal college education

- Usually at a university
- Four years of general college education, usually designated as a Bachelor of Arts Degree (BA)
- Four years of study in a specific area, usually designated as a Bachelor of Science Degree (BS)

Master's Degree
- Two to four years beyond the Bachelor's Degree
- Offered at universities
- Specialized studies with additional courses, knowledge, and skills taken after the Bachelor's Degree
- Highly specific in-depth classes, study, and research in a career, profession, or technical area
- Masters Degree is designated as Master of Arts (MA), Master of Science (MS), Master of Education (M.Ed.) Master of Fine Arts (MFA)

Specialist Degree
- Two to five years beyond the Master's Degree
- Often the precursor to entering into a Doctoral Program
- Offered at universities
- Highly specialized course of study and research
- Specialist Degree is designated as Sp.D.

Doctorate Degree
- Five or more years of study in a specialized area
- Beyond the Master's and/or Specialist Degree
- Offered at universities
- Required for most medical and mental health professionals
- Doctorate degrees can be in other specializations such as engineering, mathematics, marine science, divinity, computer science, etc.

Licensing

Licenses are issued by each state. Licenses require an individual meet specific education, training, courses, and/or work experience. The individual must graduate from an accredited institution/college/university/training program, complete an internship, pass a license examination at the state level, pay a fee, and complete periodic re-certification with college courses or continuing education units within their career field.

Licenses can be given in medical, mental, dental, veterinarians, and other health care professionals. Licenses can also be required for other types of workers including, insurance adjusters, car dealers, hair dressers/barbers, electricians, plumbers, funeral directors, law enforcement officers, firefighters, teachers, and so on.

Only those holding the appropriate state license are permitted to offer their services to the public and receive compensation. Those practicing without a license can cause great harm and can be legally prosecuted.

Certifications

Certification in a particular skill area may be issued by the state, a college, or a professional organization or association. Certification may or may not require a college degree or advanced post graduate degree.

Typically certification implies some specialized education, training, or skill recognized by those within that area of expertise.

Certification may be acquired by a specialized two year college degree such as an AA or an AS. It can also be awarded by a short training or vocational program without a college degree.

Certification may be obtained as an additional area added to credentials, above and beyond a college degree and/or a license, by a nationally recognized accreditation board. This is called "Board Certified."

CHAPTER NINE:

Hallucinations, Delusions, Illusions, Psychoses

The terms *symptoms* and *signs* are often confused and used interchangeably, however they have distinct differences.

Symptoms of mental conditions are subjective and are self-reported. They cannot be objectively observed by others. This may include such things as upset stomach, headache, tingling in extremities, feeling weak, dizziness, etc.

Signs are an objective manifestation of symptoms that result in observable behavior. Signs are observable by others, regardless of whether the individual reports them or not. This may include bleeding, vomiting, fever, fainting, and so on.

The sequence that leads to observable behaviors typically follows in this manner:

- Sensory input (seeing, hearing, feeling, tasting, smelling)

- Creation of thought

- Emotional response

- Observable behavior

- Negative signs

The *Diagnostic and Statistical Manual 5th Edition* (DSM-5) published by the *American Psychiatric Association* provides coding, classification, and diagnosis of mental disorders and is used by all licensed mental health professionals.

These are the more common *symptoms* reported by those with a mental health condition and *signs* observed by family, associates, and professionals in the mental health field.

Hallucinations are sensory experiences that seem real but are created in the mind. They can affect all five senses. They are reality based sensations, that are not actually happening, but believed to be real by the individual.

The person's belief leads to a behavioral response that is inappropriate and uncalled for in the situation. For example, the person might hear a voice no one else in the room can hear, see an image that isn't real, feel bugs crawling on their arms that are not there, or tasting an odd substance in their mouth.

Delusions relate to a firm belief the person adamantly holds as absolute truth. Delusions are defined as fixed, false beliefs that conflict with reality. Despite contrary evidence, a person in a delusional state can't let go of these convictions. Delusions are often reinforced by the misinterpretation of events. Many delusions also involve some level of paranoia and/or conspiracy theories.

Delusions are not reality based but rather sensory input believed by the individual to be real and true. These beliefs can lead to irrational behaviors which can be bizarre, dangerous, threatening or lead to harm toward self or others. Delusional beliefs often focus on grandeur, science fiction, or religious themes, such as being the true Christ, king of an empire, a world leader, a celebrity, a brilliant scientist, a successful billionaire, and so on. Frequently the focus is on the personification of objects or animals that talk, confer power, cast spells, etc.

Illusions pertain to the mind. It is a disconnect, a distortion, between perception and reality. It occurs when a sensory stimulus is present but is incorrectly perceived and misinterpreted.

An illusion is an experience that seems to originate without an external source of stimulation. It is defined as a process involving a discrepancy between one's awareness and some objective stimulus.

Illusions are a mismatch between the physical stimuli and its perception by the individual. The mismatch is caused by incorrect interpretation of information received by sense organs. Illusions can be said to "fool the mind." These are also called permanent illusions because they do not change with experience and practice. For example a person may see a large tree with long and thick limbs, however, he may believe the tree is reaching out to harm him or while watching someone adding spices as they prepare food he believes it is poison.

Everyone may occasionally experience

an illusion. However, illusions are extraordinarily common in people suffering from schizophrenia.

Psychoses is a severe mental disorder in which thought and emotions are so impaired contact is lost with external reality. In terms of what it means, a "psychotic break" with reality means losing contact with reality, such as hearing, seeing, tasting, smelling, or feeling something that has no external correlate (i.e., hallucinations) or believing something to be true that is false (i.e., a delusion) or misinterpreting and misconstruing a neutral stimulus or event (i.e., illusions.)

The outward signs of a mental condition are often behavioral. A person may be extremely quiet, sad, or withdrawn. Conversely, he or she may burst into tears, have great anxiety, or have loud outbursts of anger. Even during the course of treatment, some individuals with a mental condition can continue to exhibit anti-social behaviors.

Typically, a person will show changes in his or her behavior before psychosis develops. The list below includes several warning signs of having a psychotic episode:

<u>Early Warning Signs of Psychosis</u>

- Feeling sad or down

- Confused thinking or reduced ability to concentrate.

- Excessive fears or worries, or extreme feelings of guilt

- Extreme mood changes of highs and lows

- Withdrawal from friends and activities

- Significant tiredness, low energy, or problems sleeping

- A lack of interest or motivation in social activities

- Irritable, overly sensitive, argumentative

- Verbal outbursts, aggressive behavior

- Threats or intimidation toward others

- Direct or indirect suicidal intentions or attempts

- Worrisome drop in grades or job performance

- Suspiciousness, paranoid ideas, thoughts of conspiracies, or plans of being harmed by others

- Uneasiness being with others or in crowds

- Withdrawing socially, spending more time alone than usual

- Unusual, overly intense new ideas

- Strange feelings or having no feelings at all, or emotional numbing.

- Decline in self-care or personal hygiene

- Difficulty telling reality from fantasy

- Confused speech or trouble communicating

CHAPTER TEN:

Mood Disorders

Mood disorder is a broad term used to include all the different types of depressive and bipolar disorders, both of which affect mood. Mood disorders cause major changes in one's emotional state and are manifest in extreme changes in behavior. A person can experience deep depression and then not long after experience excited mania.

Mood disorders have a severe impact on the individual and can cause a life filled with sadness, fear, or insecurity. In some instances, mood disorders can lead to suicide.

The emotional state of those with a mood disorder is distorted or inconsistent with their circumstances and interferes with their ability to function appropriately. The person may be extremely sad, emotionally empty, or irritable (depressed), or may have periods of depression alternating with being excessively happy (mania).

Mania is a condition in which the person is basically 'too happy.' Everything can seem perfectly fine to him or her, even when, in reality, things are not going well. They may also find they have seemingly endless energy. They struggle to control their impulses. They present with higher levels of novelty seeking behaviors, and lower levels of self-directedness, and a limited ability to be cooperative.

Psychotherapy and medication are used to try to create a balance between depression and mania. Medication does not cure mental conditions but helps to regulate signs symptoms.

Some of the most common mood disorders that affect people all over the world include major depressive disorder, dysthymic disorder, bipolar disorder, mood disorder due to a general medical condition, and substance-induced mood disorder.

- **Major Depressive Disorder (MDD)—** prolonged and persistent periods of extreme sadness. Limited interests, no motivation, extreme fatigue, a change in weight, sleep problems, psychomotor agitation or retardation, feeling worthless, inappropriate feelings of guilt, difficulty with concentration, inability to make decisions, thoughts of death and/or dying, suicidal ideation, suicide attempts, and/or a suicide plan.

- **Bipolar Disorder**—also known as manic-depression, or affective disorder, is one of the best known of all mood disorders. It is characterized by extreme mood swings which include alternating times of depression and mania.

- **Seasonal Affective Disorder (SAD)**—a form of depression most often associated with fewer hours of daylight in the far northern and southern latitudes from late fall to early spring. It may also impact those employed where irregular shift work is required.

- **Cyclothymic Disorder**—a disorder that causes emotional ups and downs that are less extreme than bipolar disorder

- **Premenstrual Dysphoric Disorder**— mood changes and irritability that occur during the premenstrual phase of a woman's cycle and go away with the onset of menses

- **Persistent Depressive Disorder (dysthymia)**—a long-term (chronic) form of depression.

- **Disruptive Mood Dysregulation Disorder**—a disorder of chronic, severe, and persistent irritability in children that often includes frequent temper outbursts that are inconsistent with the child's developmental age.

- **Depression Related to Medical Illness** —a persistent depressed mood with a significant loss of pleasure in most or all activities and little motivation that's directly related to the physical effects of a medical condition

- **Depression Induced by Substance Use/Abuse or Prescribed Medication.** The depressive symptoms began soon after the introduction or soon after the withdrawal of the medication, substance or intoxicant.

CHAPTER ELEVEN:

Anxiety Disorders

Anxiety is a feeling of fear, dread, and uneasiness, and can lead to the development of feelings like hopelessness. It affects mood, but it is not considered a mood disorder because it is not directly related to mood. Anxiety disorders are generally treated with psychotherapy, medication, stress management techniques, and support groups.

Anxiety might cause you to sweat, feel restless and tense, and have a rapid heartbeat. Anxiety can be a normal stress reaction. For example, you might feel anxious when faced with a difficult problem at work, before taking a test, or before making an important decision.

Common signs and symptoms of anxiety can include:

- Feeling nervous, restless or tense

- A sense of impending danger, panic or doom

- An increased heart rate

- Breathing rapidly (hyperventilation)

- Sweating

- Trembling

- Feeling weak or tired

- Trouble concentrating or thinking about anything other than the present worry

- Trouble with sleep on-set and/or awakening

- Experiencing gastrointestinal (GI) problems

- Difficulty controlling worry

- The urge to avoid things, people, or situations that may trigger anxiety

There are several types of anxiety disorders, including generalized anxiety disorder, panic disorder, and various phobia-related disorders. Anxiety disorders include:

- **Agoraphobia** (ag-uh-ruh-FOE-be-uh) disorder in which the person experiences fear and often avoids places or situations that might cause panic and feeling trapped, helpless, or embarrassed. This may include using public transportation, being in open spaces or enclosed spaces, standing in line or being in a crowd, or being alone outside of his/her home.

- **Anxiety Disorder** due to a medical condition includes symptoms of intense anxiety or panic that are directly caused by a physical health problem.

- **Generalized Anxiety Disorder** (GAD) includes persistent and excessive anxiety and worry about activities or events — even ordinary, routine issues. The worry is out of proportion to the actual circumstance, is difficult to control and can result in physical symptoms. It often occurs with other anxiety disorders or depression.

- **Obsessive-Compulsive Disorder** (OCD) is characterized by uncontrollable, recurring thoughts (obsessions) that can lead people to engage in repetitive behaviors (compulsions) in an effort to ward off their high levels of anxiety.

- **Panic Disorder** involves repeated episodes of sudden feelings of intense anxiety and fear or terror that reach a peak within minutes (panic attacks). It may include feelings of impending doom, shortness of breath, chest pain, or a rapid, fluttering or pounding heart (heart palpitations). Panic attacks may lead to worry or fear about them happening again or avoiding situations in which they've occurred.

- **Selective Mutism** is a consistent failure of children, and in some adults, to speak in certain situations, such as school or work, even when they can speak in other situations, such as at home with close family members. This can interfere with social functioning. Selective mutism usually occurs before the age of five and is often associated with extreme shyness, fear of social embarrassment, compulsive traits, withdrawal, clinging behavior, and temper tantrums. People diagnosed with selective mutism are often also diagnosed with other anxiety disorders.

- **Separation Anxiety** disorder is typically a childhood disorder, but can be experienced by adults, characterized by anxiety that's excessive for the child's developmental level and related to separation from parents or others who have parental roles. They often worry some sort of harm or something untoward will happen to their attachment figures while they are separated. This fear leads them to avoid being separated from their attachment figures and to avoid being alone. People with separation anxiety may have nightmares about being separated from those they trust or experience physical symptoms when separation occurs or is anticipated.

- **Social Anxiety Disorder** (social phobia) involves high levels of anxiety, fear, and avoidance of social situations due to feelings of embarrassment, self-consciousness, and concern about being judged or viewed negatively by others. It is a general intense fear of, or anxiety toward, social or performance situations. This worry often causes people to avoid social situations and may lead to isolation.

- **Specific Phobias**, sometimes called simple phobias, are characterized as an intense fear of—or aversion to—specific objects, people, or situations. Phobias cause an irrational or excessive worry about encountering the feared object or situation. Although it can be realistic to be anxious in some circumstances, the intensity of fear with a phobia is out of proportion to the actual danger caused by the situation or object. Phobias provoke panic attacks in some people.

- **Substance-induced Anxiety Disorder** is characterized by symptoms of intense anxiety or panic that are a direct result of misusing drugs, taking medications, being exposed to a toxic substance, or withdrawal from drugs.

Other specified anxiety disorders and unspecified anxiety disorders are terms for anxiety or phobias that don't meet the exact criteria for any other anxiety disorders but are significant enough to be distressing and disruptive.

Risk Factors

Researchers are finding that both genetic and environmental factors contribute to the risk of developing an anxiety disorder.

Although the risk factors for each type of anxiety disorder can vary, some general risk factors for all types of anxiety disorders include:

- Temperamental traits of shyness or behavioral inhibition in childhood

- Exposure to stressful and negative life or environmental events in early childhood or adulthood

- A history of anxiety or other mental illnesses in biological relatives

- Some physical health conditions, such as thyroid problems or heart arrhythmias. Caffeine or other substances, or medical issues can produce or aggravate anxiety symptoms.

Treatment Modalities

Medication

Medication does not cure anxiety disorders but can help relieve signs and symptoms. Medication for anxiety is prescribed by a psychiatrist or primary care provider. Some states allow psychologists who have received specialized training to prescribe psychiatric medications.

Certain substances such as caffeine, some over-the-counter cold medicines, illicit drugs, and herbal supplements may aggravate the symptoms of anxiety disorders or interact negatively with prescribed medication.

The most common classes of medications used to combat anxiety disorders are anti-anxiety drugs (such as benzodiazepines), anti-depressants, and beta-blockers.

<u>Anti-anxiety</u>

Anti-anxiety medications can help reduce the symptoms of anxiety, panic attacks, or extreme fear and worry. The most common anti-anxiety medications are called benzodiazepines.

Although benzodiazepines are sometimes used as first-line treatments for generalized anxiety disorder, they have benefits and drawbacks.

Some benefits of benzodiazepines are their effectiveness in relieving anxiety and they take effect more quickly than antidepressant medications which are often prescribed for anxiety. Some drawbacks of benzodiazepines are people can build up a tolerance to them and may need higher and higher doses to get the same effect. Some people may even become dependent on them. Physicians usually prescribe benzodiazepines for short periods of time, which is especially helpful for older adults who may be taking other medications, people who have substance abuse problems, and people who become dependent on medication easily.

If people suddenly stop taking benzodiazepines, they may have withdrawal symptoms, or their anxiety may return. Benzodiazepines should be tapered off slowly.

For long-term use, benzodiazepines are often considered a second-line treatment for anxiety (with antidepressants being considered a first-line treatment) as well as an "as-needed" treatment for any distressing flare-up of symptoms.

A different type of anti-anxiety medication is buspirone. Buspirone is a non-benzodiazepine medication specifically indicated for the treatment of chronic anxiety, although it does not help everyone.

Anti-depressants

Antidepressants are used to treat depression, but they can also be helpful for treating anxiety disorders. They may help improve the way the brain uses certain chemicals that control mood or stress. Several different antidepressant medicines may need to be tried before finding the one that relieves signs and symptoms and has manageable side effects.

Antidepressants can take time to work, so it's important to give the medication a chance before reaching a conclusion about its effectiveness. Stopping them abruptly can cause withdrawal symptoms.

Antidepressants called selective serotonin reuptake inhibitors (SSRIs) and serotonin-norepinephrine reuptake inhibitors (SNRIs) are commonly used as first-line treatments for anxiety. Less commonly used, but effective treatments for anxiety disorders, are older classes of antidepressants, such as tricyclic antidepressants and monoamine oxidase inhibitors (MAOIs).

In some cases, children, teenagers, and young adults under 25 may experience an increase in suicidal thoughts or behavior when taking antidepressant medications, especially in the first few weeks after starting or when the dose is changed. Patients of all ages taking antidepressants should be monitored closely, especially during the first few weeks of treatment.

Beta-Blockers

Although beta-blockers are most often used to treat high blood pressure, they can also be used to help relieve the physical signs of anxiety, such as rapid heartbeat, shaking, trembling, and blushing. These medications, when taken for a short period of time, can help keep physical signs and symptoms under control. They can also be used "as needed" to reduce acute anxiety, including as a preventive intervention for some predictable forms of performance anxieties.

Stress Management Techniques

Stress management techniques and meditation can help people with anxiety disorders calm themselves and may enhance the effects of therapy. Research suggests aerobic exercise can help some people manage their anxiety; however, exercise should not take the place of standard care and more research is needed. Other helpful relaxation techniques include engagement with a wide social group, pursuing hobbies and interests, frequent walks, healthy dietary habits, breathing exercises, and reading.

Support Groups

Some people with anxiety disorders might benefit from joining a self-help or support group and sharing their concerns and achievements with others. Internet chat rooms might also be useful, but any advice received over the internet should be used with caution, as online acquaintances have usually never met each other and what has helped one person is not necessarily what is best for another.

CHAPTER TWELVE:

Personality Disorders

A personality disorder is a type of mental disorder with a rigid and unhealthy pattern of thinking, functioning and behaving. The person has trouble perceiving and relating to situations and people. This causes significant problems and limitations in relationships, social activities, work and school.

Personality is the combination of thoughts, emotions and behaviors that makes us unique. It's the way we view, understand and relate to the outside world, as well as how we see ourselves. Personality forms during childhood, and is shaped through the interaction of genetic factors and our environment. Sometimes this is referred to as our "temperament."

Although the precise cause of personality disorders is not known, certain factors seem to increase the risk of developing or triggering personality disorders, including:

- Family history of personality disorders

- Family members diagnosed with a mental illness

- Abusive, unstable or chaotic family life during childhood

- Being diagnosed with childhood conduct disorder

- Variations in brain chemistry and structure

In some cases, individuals may not realize they have a personality disorder because their way of thinking and behaving seems natural to them. Typically, they blame others for the challenges they face.

Personality disorders usually begin in the teenage years or early adulthood. There are many types of personality disorders. Some types may become less obvious as the person ages.

Types of personality disorders are grouped into three clusters, based on similar characteristics and symptoms. Many people with one personality disorder also have signs and symptoms of at least one additional personality disorder. It's not necessary to exhibit all the signs and symptoms listed for a disorder to be diagnosed.

CLUSTER "A" PERSONALITY DISORDERS

Cluster A personality disorders are characterized by odd, eccentric thinking or behavior. They include paranoid personality, schizoid personality disorder and schizotypal personality disorder.

Paranoid Personality Disorder

Pervasive distrust and suspicion of others and their motives

- Unjustified belief that others are trying to harm or deceive them

- Unjustified suspicion of the loyalty or trustworthiness of others

- Hesitancy to confide in others due to unreasonable fear that others will use the information against them

- Perception of innocent remarks or nonthreatening situations as personal insults or attacks

- Angry or hostile reaction to perceived slights or insults

- Tendency to hold grudges

- Unjustified, recurrent suspicion that spouse or sexual partner is unfaithful

Schizoid Personality Disorder

- Lack of interest in social or personal relationships, preferring to be alone

- Limited range of emotional expression

- Inability to take pleasure in most activities

- Inability to pick up normal social cues

- Appearance of being cold or indifferent to others

- Little or no interest in having sex with another person

Schizotypal Personality Disorder

- Peculiar dress, thinking, beliefs, speech or behavior

- Odd perceptual experiences, such as hearing a voice whisper your name

- Flat emotions or inappropriate emotional responses

- Social anxiety and a lack of or discomfort with close relationships

- Indifferent, inappropriate or suspicious response to others

- "Magical thinking"—believing they can influence people and events with their thoughts

- Belief that certain casual incidents or events have hidden messages meant only for them

CLUSTER "B" PERSONALITY DISORDERS

Cluster B personality disorders are characterized by dramatic, overly emotional or unpredictable thinking or behavior. They include antisocial personality disorder, borderline personality disorder, histrionic personality disorder and narcissistic personality disorder.

Antisocial Personality Disorder

- Disregard for others' needs or feelings

- Persistent lying, stealing, aliases, conning others

- Recurring problems with the law

- Repeated violation of the rights of others

- Aggressive, often violent behavior

- Disregard for the safety of self or others

- Impulsive behavior

- Consistently irresponsible

- Lack of remorse for behavior

Borderline Personality Disorder

- Impulsive and risky behavior, such as having unsafe sex, gambling or binge eating

- Unstable or fragile self-image

- Unstable and intense relationships

- Up and down moods, often as a reaction to interpersonal stress

- Suicidal behavior or threats of self-injury

- Intense fear of being alone or abandoned

- Ongoing feelings of emptiness

- Frequent, intense displays of anger

- Stress-related paranoia that comes and goes

Histrionic Personality Disorder

- Constantly seeking attention

- Excessively emotional, dramatic or sexually provocative to gain attention

- Speaks dramatically with strong opinions, but few facts or details to back them up

- Easily influenced by others

- Shallow, rapidly changing emotions

- Excessive concern with physical appearance

- Thinks relationships with others are closer than they really are

Narcissistic Personality Disorder

- Belief that they're special and more important than others

- Fantasies about power, success and attractiveness

- Failure to recognize others' needs and feelings

- Exaggeration of achievements or talents

- Expectation of constant praise and admiration

- Arrogance

- Unreasonable expectations of favors and advantages, often taking advantage of others

- Envy of others or belief that others envy them

<u>CLUSTER "C" PERSONALITY DISORDERS</u>

Cluster C personality disorders are characterized by anxious, fearful thinking or behavior. They include avoidant personality disorder, dependent personality disorder and obsessive-compulsive personality disorder.

Avoidant Personality Disorder

- Overly sensitive to criticism or rejection

- Feeling inadequate, inferior or unattractive

- Avoidance of work activities that require interpersonal contact

- Socially inhibited, timid and isolated, avoiding new activities or meeting strangers

- Extreme shyness in social situations and personal relationships

- Fear of disapproval, embarrassment or ridicule

Dependent Personality Disorder

- Excessive dependence on others and feeling the need to be taken care of

- Submissive or clingy behavior toward others

- Fear of having to provide self-care or fend for themselves if left alone

- Lack of self-confidence, requiring excessive advice and reassurance from others to make even small decisions

- Difficulty starting or doing projects on your own due to lack of self-confidence

- Difficulty disagreeing with others, fearing disapproval

- Tolerance of poor or abusive treatment, even when other options are available

- Urgent need to start a new relationship when a close one has ended

Obsessive-Compulsive Personality Disorder

- Preoccupation with details, orderliness and rules

- Extreme perfectionism, resulting in dysfunction and distress when perfection is not achieved, such as feeling unable to finish a project because they don't meet their own strict standards

- Desire to be in control of people, tasks and situations, and inability to delegate tasks

- Neglect of friends and enjoyable activities because of excessive commitment to work or a project

- Inability to discard broken or worthless objects

- Rigid and stubborn

- Inflexible about morality, ethics or values

- Tight, miserly control over budgeting and spending money

CHAPTER THIRTEEN:

Thought Disorders

Thought disorder is a disorganized way of thinking that leads to abnormal ways of expressing language when speaking and writing. It's one of the primary symptoms of schizophrenia, but it may be present in other mental disorders such as mania and depression.

Thought disorder is one of the most difficult mental disorders to diagnose and treat, as many people exhibit symptoms of thought disorder occasionally. Some people may demonstrate thought disorder only when they're tired.

Each type of thought disorder has unique symptoms. However, a disruption in the interconnectivity of ideas is present in all types.

Even though it's common for most people to display some of the symptoms of thought disorder occasionally, thought disorder isn't classified until it negatively affects the ability to communicate.

Although there are more than 20 sub-types of thought disorders, some of the most common types are:

Alogia

People with alogia, also known as poverty of speech, give brief and unelaborated responses to questions. People with this form of thought disorder rarely speak unless prompted. Alogia is often seen in people with dementia or schizophrenia.

Blocking

People with thought blocking often interrupt themselves abruptly mid-sentence. They might pause for several seconds or minutes. When they start talking again, they often change the topic of conversation. Thought blocking is common in people with schizophrenia.

Circumstantiality

People with circumstantiality, also known as circumstantial thinking, or circumstantial speech, often include excessive irrelevant details in their speaking or writing. They maintain their original train of thought but provide a lot of unnecessary details before circling back to their main point.

Clanging or clang association

A person with clang association makes word choices based on the sound of the word rather than the meaning of the word. They may rely on using rhymes, alliterations, or puns and create sentences that don't make sense. Clanging thought process is a common symptom of mania.

Derailment

A person with derailment talks in chains of only semi-related ideas. Their ideas often fall further and further from the topic of conversation. For example, people with derailment thought disorder might jump from talking about rabbits (hares), to the hair on their head, to your fuzzy sweater.

Distractible Speech

A person with distractible speech thought disorder has trouble maintaining a topic. They shift quickly between topics and get distracted by internal and external stimuli. It's commonly seen in people with mania. For example, somebody exhibiting distractible speech might abruptly ask where you got your hat mid-sentence while telling you about a recent vacation.

Echolalia

People with echolalia struggle to communicate. They often repeat noises and words they hear instead of expressing their thoughts. For example, instead of answering a question, they may repeat the question.

CHAPTER FOURTEEN:

Special Populations

Roughly half of all lifetime mental disorders manifest signs and symptoms in the mid-teenage group. Three-fourths of those with mental disorders are individuals diagnosed while in their mid-20s. Later onset of mental disorders are usually due to secondary conditions. Severe mental disorders are typically preceded by less severe disorders that are rarely brought to clinical attention.

Specific consideration is given to treating those within special populations. Listed are a few situations where individuals are categorized as "high risk" or with "special needs."

Dual Diagnosis: Mental Illness and Substance Abuse

Dual diagnosis is a combination of mental illness and substance use/abuse. Dual diagnosis is sometimes referred to as co-occurring disorders or co-morbidity. The term "co-morbidity" describes two or more disorders occurring in the same person. They can occur at the same time or one after the other. Co-morbidity also implies interactions between the illnesses that can worsen the course of both. According to the National Survey on Drug Use and Health, 9.5 million U.S. adults experienced both mental illness and a substance use disorder in 2019.

Young Children and Adolescents

Children from birth to age 10 are considered "children of tender years." At this young age, children are unable to reasonable care for themselves or make sound decisions about their safety and well-being. They are vulnerable to the whims of those in a position of authority. They often suffer abuse, neglect, lack of medical care, and limited social support due to the beliefs and behavior of caregivers and/or wrongdoers.

Preteens and adolescents are aged 11 to 18. Although they continue to need support and monitoring, they often come to harm at the hands of their peers or with high risk and/or self-injurious behaviors.

Their ability to consider alternatives is limited and their decision making can be poor. Even when provided with love and support, they are often uncooperative with efforts for good health habits, nutrition, safety, and positive social involvement.

It is during these years when a mental health diagnosis is often first made.

Accompanying a diagnosis there is typically a recommendation by a physician or mental health care professional for a combination of therapy and medication if warranted. However, this is also the age of self-determination and the development of a unique personal identity. These factors often lead to resistance by the teenager and a lack of cooperation with those attempting to provide help.

Conditions diagnosed in childhood include:

- Attention-deficit Hyperactivity Disorder

- Autism Spectrum Disorder /Asperger's

- Conduct Disorder

- Oppositional-Defiant Disorder

- Tourette's Syndrome

Children are often identified as they struggle academically, have poor peer relationships, or unusual behaviors. The educational system is geared to identify, evaluate, and provide services via an *Exceptional Student Education Program* (ESE). An *Individual Education Plan* (IEP) will be developed to address academic, social, medical, and mental health care. If the child's disability is primarily medical, such as Type I Diabetes, Spina Bifida, Blindness, Deafness, and so on the IEP is often written to provide services for *Other Health Impaired*(OHI). An IEP only covers services until the child completes 12th grade.

Those With Disabilities and/or Chronic Medical Conditions

Individuals may be born with conditions which present with a lifelong need for medical and mental health care. Others may develop a disease or illness as they age. Additionally, there are those with lifelong injuries from accidents or traumatic experiences.

Often medical conditions, multiple hospitalizations, continuing care, limitations of physical functioning, medications and side effects, as well as the use of medical equipment impacts the person's emotional state. Depression and anxiety are frequent diagnoses for those in these situations.

Dependent Adults

Those over the age of 18 who have a documented medical condition or mental disorder may have a *504 Plan*. This is based on Federal Law and requires reasonable accommodations in school, the workplace, and the community.

These individuals often have a legal guardian to monitor and offer support with activities of daily living (ADL), legal issues, and appropriate living conditions. This is a high risk group as most of these individuals are under medical care and taking prescribed medications. If they have a limited ability to comply with care and/or their medication regime, it could lead to adverse or allergic reactions which manifest in unusual thinking and/or behaviors.

Elderly Population

The risk of medical conditions, use of multiple medications, and physical limitations make elderly individuals a vulnerable population. They often live alone and self care may be limited leading to malnutrition, injuries, and lack of appropriate medical care.

Many elderly people are able to carry on normal lives within an Adult Living Facility. Typically this is independent living within a designated community. Various services are available including housekeeping, meals, social activities, and medical services as needed.

Those with limited mental capacity or severe mental or physical conditions may be more suited for a Skilled Nursing Facility (SNF). This is a higher level of care, including everything necessary for Activities of Daily Living and continuous levels of medical care as needed.

Elderly persons are vulnerable and can be harmed by caregivers or neglected by family members. In an effort to preserve their independence they may become uncooperative with efforts of assistance and protection.

CHAPTER: FIFTEEN

Strategies for Positive Interactions

The goal when interacting with those who have mental health conditions is for all involved to be safe and free of harm to themselves or others. Every effort should be made to resolve the immediate situation without force and quickly obtain appropriate medical and/or mental health services. The focus of interactions should be to respect, understand, and deal with the individual's confused state of mind, and perhaps, his or her hostile thoughts and actions.

OBSERVATIONS

- Observe for weapons or items in the locale that could be used to do harm

- Be aware of on-lookers who might try to assist or those who might be opposed to your help

- Assess the individual's stance, clothing, facial expression, eye contact

- Observe their ability to stand and move without assistance

- Look for signs of alcohol or drug use/abuse
- Look for obvious injuries or wounds

- Listen to their speech for slurred words, confused statements, illogical or irrational comments

- Listen to the content of their words and speech patterns for threats, suicide ideation, hallucinations, delusions, or illusions

- Consider their explanation of any medical conditions, medications, or names of treating professionals

VERBAL RESPONSES

- Speak in a steady voice that projects control over the situation

- Use a firm but calm tone; do not shout or yell unless necessary to get their attention
- Do not belittle, name call, disrespect, or humiliate

- Give single-step directions

- Use direct commands

- Limit questioning to personal identity, family information, medical conditions, medications, illness, injuries, names of treating professionals

- Allow the opportunity for them to explain their version of the situation or events leading up to it. Accept what they say without questioning the accuracy, truthfulness or the logic of their response

- Be logical, try "if-then" scenarios, encourage them to consider alternative behaviors. Avoid blame, shame, and criticism
- Patiently explain who you are, what your role is, and what will happen next

PHYSICAL

- Keep a safe distance away

- Give them their personal space

- Keep them from approaching too closely

- Do not make sudden moves or gestures

- Allow them to pace or flail their arms within reason

- If they become aggressive or violent or threaten harm, do not try to restrain them. Do not get physical with them. Do not brandish a weapon or an item that can be used as a weapon or for self defense. **Leave the area and call 911.**

INDEX

DSM-5	*Diagnostic and Statistical Manual - 5th Ed.*
DX	Diagnosis
ESE	Exceptional Student Education
HOI	Other Health Impaired
IEP	Individual Educational Plan
HX	History
ICD	International Classification of Disease
LEA	Local Education Agency
LCSW	Licensed Clinical Social Worker
LMFT	Licensed Marriage and Family Therapist
LMHC	Licensed Mental Health Counselor
NIH	National Institute of Health

NIMH	National Institute of Mental Health
NORD	National Organization of Rare Disorders
NSDUH	National Survey on Drug Use & Health
OTC	Over the Counter (Medications)
PDR	Physician's Desk Reference
RX	Prescribed Medication
SAMHSA	Substance Abuse & Mental Health Services Administration
SNF	Skilled Nursing Facility
TTY (TT)	Telecommunication Device for the Deaf
TX	Treatment
WHO	World Health Organization

RESOURCES

DSM–5	*Diagnostic & Statistical Manual-5*
Domestic Violence	1 (800) 799-7233
Emergency Services	911
LGBTQ	1 (866) 488-7386
NIMH	1 (866) 615-6464
PDR	*Physician's Desk Reference*
SAMHSA.gov	1 (800) 662-4357
Suicide Hotline	1 (800) 273-8255

About the Author

Valerie Allen, Ed.D. NCSP, CCM is a psychologist, case manager, and author. She has been in private practice for more than 30 years. She specializes in working with young children, adolescents, and their parents. She works with those in alternative family settings and life styles.

She has taught students in elementary, high school, and college. She has also taught those in undergraduate and graduate university programs. She has served as an academic adviser for counselor/mental health graduate education programs and as a director of teacher education programs.

She conducts seminars for educators, parents, medical, and mental health professionals based on her motivational, self-help books, *Beyond the Inkblots: Confusion to Harmony* and *Understanding Mental Illness: A Guide for Family and Friends.*

She is a member of the *Florida Association of School Psychologists* and Board Certified by the *National Association of School Psychologists*. She is also a *Certified Case Manager* by *The National Commission on Case Management*. She is a first responder for *Critical Incident Stress Debriefing and Terrorism.*

She lives in warm and sunny Florida, where she has raised six children from whom she has learned many things about life and love.

She can be contacted at DrVAllen.com and DrValerieAllen@cs.com